memorise

WWW.FORTYFIVE.ONE
#ATOZBIBLE

memorise

INTRODUCTION
#ATO**Z**BIBLE

I had never struggled with sleep but recently found myself in a season of wakefulness and, in those dark nights, I was aware of a disquiet in my soul and in my mind. It was as if fear and anxiety thought it was ok to take hold ... it wasn't! In the night it felt as though there was very little I could do but pray and cling on to Christ; hoping for sleep. In the morning there was hope and there was also space for action.

I realised that despite over thirty years of faith I had very little certainty in my night-time arsenal! I had so little scripture in reserve with which to put up adequate defence. I knew the Lord was my rock, my fortress and my deliverance but I couldn't prove it to myself or any attacker! I had a wealth of awareness and lyric but very little referenced fact.

In the quiet of day I decided to do something about it. I committed that in the calm I would prepare myself for any storm. I would arm myself with truth. Inspired by a YouTube video posted by Pablo Izquierdo entitled, 'Cute little boy impressively recites A to Z Bible verses' I found the shape and strategy of my defence.

What a joy then came as a father. Not only had I memorised a well of truth for myself to sleep by, but, when a couple of months later, my eldest daughter was finding it impossible to settle herself at night, I had an overflow of truth for her too. I was able to give verses of encouragement for her to meditate on and recite as she went to sleep. She has rarely been disturbed or unsettled since that first night and if she is, together we return to the verses.

This alphabet of truth is focussed on the joy of God, his delight in us as his children, and his intimacy with us.

In the first part of the book there are two 'levels' of memorisation and meditation. The bold words are the simple truths that even very young children can commit to memory. The fuller verses and scripture references are perhaps harder but well worth the effort to learn. We found that it was easiest to learn the short versions first and then work our way back through the alphabet using the short version as a framework and guide for the full verse.

A number of years ago I had the privilege of working on some resources with BUild (Baptist Union initiative with people with learning disabilities).They had created versions of the Creed and the Lord's prayer to use with simple actions. Inspired by them I have created corresponding actions, with a single word or two, alongside each verse. Each action flows one to the next so, these movements can be used to help remember the verses or as a way of expressing the truth without speaking.

More resources at *fortyfive.one* This book has further options for learning, reciting and meditating on scripture available online. For example **a series of stretches** that can be used in the morning, before bed or as part of your exercise routine and **'You are creative'** which is a way to engage creatively with these truths.

Whenever I can't sleep or feel anxious, I begin to recite under my breath or silently in my Spirit. I begin with, 'Abide in me' and allow each truth to fill my mind. Sometimes I keep going and work through the alphabet, other times I will linger on a singer verse or word as I explore the truth and allow the reality to take hold.

However you use this book I pray that the truth will flood your memory, your nights and your days and that it will be a blessing to you and you entire family.

memorise

#**A**TO**Z**BIBLE

CONTENTS

more resources available at
www.fortyfive.one

memorise

AN A-Z OF VERSES TO SLEEP & LIVE BY
CURATED BY JASON JOHN HUFFADINE
#ATOZBIBLE

ABIDE

With your left hand make a shape as if you are holding a glass. Put the four fingers of your right hand into the opening

Abide in me, and I in you. As the branch cannot bear fruit by itself, unless it abides in the vine, neither can you, unless you abide in me.

John 15:4 ESV

BE STILL

Twist your hands outwards and upwards so that your palms face away from you with your fingers spread out in a stop pose

Be still, and know that I am God.

I will be exalted among the nations,

I will be exalted in the earth!

Psalm 46:10 ESV

COME

Turn your hands towards your face, keeping your hands in the same place pull your fingers towards your face to say, "Come"

Come to me, all you who

are weary and burdened,

and I will give you rest.

Matthew 11:28 NIV

DRAW NEAR

Close your hands to a fist. Stretch out your
index (pointing) fingers and move your hands
so that your two index fingertips touch

Draw near to God, and he will draw near to you. Cleanse your hands, you sinners, and purify your hearts, you double-minded.

James 4:8 ESV

ENTER

Let you fingers spread out again and twist your
hands outwards so your palms face away from
each other as if clearing the way to move forward

Enter his gates with thanksgiving

and his courts with praise; give

thanks to him and praise his name.

Psalm 100:4 NIV

FIX

Hold your middle and index finger together. Start with your hand near to your eye, then follow your hand up and away as you move it away from your face

Let us fix our eyes on Jesus, the author and perfecter of our faith, who for the joy set before Him endured the cross, scorning its shame, and sat down at the right hand of the throne of God.

Hebrews 12:2 BSB

GIVE

Hold you hands in front of you as if holding something small and precious. Move your hands forwards as if giving that thing away

Give thanks to the LORD, for

he is good! His faithful love

endures forever.

Psalm 107:1 NLT

HOW LOVELY

Roll one hand over the other to turn both hands palm down. Pull your hands apart until they make an arch and now press your fingertips together to make a roof

How lovely is your dwelling place,

O LORD of Heaven's Armies.

Psalm 84:1 NLT

I AM

Separate your hands and point with both of them
to the sky and allow your gaze to follow your
fingers to look up

I am the LORD your God;

consecrate yourselves and be holy,

because I am holy.

Leviticus 11:44a NIV

JOY

Use one hand to make a 'v' with your forefinger and thumb. Move your hand up across your mouth like a smile of joy. You may want to repeat the motion

Nehemiah said, "Go and enjoy choice food and sweet drinks, and send some to those who have nothing prepared. This day is holy to our Lord. Do not grieve, for **the joy of the LORD is your strength.**

Nehemiah 8:10 NIV

KING

Make your hands flat as if you are going to clap and put your hands up as close to the side of your head as you can to make a crown

On his robe and on his

thigh he has a name written,

King of kings and Lord of lords.

Revelation 19:16 ESV

LORD
ROCK / FORTRESS / DELIVERER

There are three actions for this verse.

Rock: two fists one on top of the other

Fortress: palms of your hands covering your face

Deliverer: hands dropped before you as if God is holding you in the palm of his hand

The LORD is my rock and my fortress and my deliverer, my God, my rock, in whom I take refuge, my shield, and the horn of my salvation, my stronghold.

Psalm 18:2 NIV

MY HEART

Use one or both of your hands to cover your heart

My soul longs, yes, faints

for the courts of the LORD;

my heart and flesh sing for joy

to the living God.

Psalm 84:2 ESV

NOTHING

Make an 'x' with your forefingers and hold them in
front of your mouth as you recite the verse

"For **nothing will be impossible with God."** And Mary said, "Behold, I am the servant of the Lord; let it be to me according to your word."

Luke 1:37-38a ESV

OH, CLAP!

Clap your hands together once or repeatedly as you recite the verse

Oh, clap your hands, all you peoples! Shout to God with the voice of triumph! For the LORD Most High is awesome; He is a great King over all the earth.

Psalm 47:1-2 NKJV

PREPARE

Start with your fists clenched close to your body
and then move them forwards, opening your
hands and spreading them out

A voice cries: "In the wilderness

prepare the way of the LORD;

make straight in the desert a

highway for our God.

Isaiah 40:3 ESV

QUENCH

Cover your mouth

Do not quench the Spirit.

1 Thessalonians 5:19 NIV

REMEMBER

Put your hands up to your head and as you recite
the verse speak to your mind. Tell yourself to
remember the wonders God has done

Remember the wonders he

has done, his miracles, and the

judgments he pronounced,

1 Chronicles 16:12 NIV

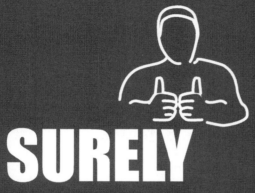

SURELY

Put your thumbs then pass one hand over the other and the other and repeat in a forward motion to indicate God's goodness following you

Surely your goodness and love will follow me all the days of my life, and I will dwell in the house of the LORD forever.

Psalm 23:6 NIV

THIS IS

Hold your hands open before you. Look at your hands and imagine that everything of the day is there. Choose to be thankful and rejoice

This is the day that the LORD has made; let us rejoice and be glad in it.

Psalm 118:24 ESV

UNDER

Cover your head with your hands.
As you lift your hands imagine God
lifting his protection over you

He will cover you with his feathers, and **under his wings you will find refuge**; his faithfulness will be your shield and rampart

Psalm 91:4 NIV

VICTORY

Strike your best victory pose. Tense your muscles
and feel the strength of God and his victory

The horse is made ready for the

day of battle, but the

victory belongs to the LORD.

Proverbs 21:31 ESV

WORTHY

Spread out your fingers and cross your
hands together so that your fingers interlock.
This is a 'w' in sign language

In a loud voice they were saying: "**Worthy is the Lamb**, who was slain to receive power and wealth and wisdom and strength and honour and glory and praise!"

Revelation 5:12 NIV

EXCELLENT

Now make an 'x' with your arms. You may want
to raise your arms higher for the second half
of the verse

O LORD, our Lord,

How excellent is Your name in

all the earth, Who have set Your

glory above the heavens!

Psalm 8:1 NKJV

YOURS

Make 'L's with you thumbs and forefingers this is one way to sign, Lord. But we're going to also use this position to point up for the word, 'yours'

Yours, O LORD is the greatness

and the power and the glory and the

victory and the majesty, for all that is in

the heavens and in the earth is yours.

Yours is the kingdom, O LORD and you

are exalted as head above all.

1 Chronicles 29:11 ESV

Zzz!

This verse is about finding rest and peace in the storm and the victory of Jesus over the storm. Put your finger over your lips as if saying, "shhh!" to quieten yourself and to quieten the storm in the name of Jesus

Suddenly a furious storm came up on the lake, so that the waves swept over the boat. But Jesus was sleeping. The disciples went and woke him, saying, "Lord, save us! We're going to drown!" He replied, "You of little faith, why are you so afraid?" Then he got up and rebuked the winds and the waves, **and it was completely calm.**

Matthew 8:24-26 NIV

DRAW NEAR
ENTER
FIX
GIVE
KING
LORD ROCK
LORD FORTRESS
LORD DELIVERER
QUENCH
REMEMBER
SURELY
THIS IS
EXCELLENT
YOURS
Zzz!

A **Abide** in me, and I in you

B **Be still**, and know that I am God

C **Come** to me ... and I will give you rest

D **Draw near** to God, and he will draw near to you

E **Enter** his gates with thanksgiving and his courts with praise

F Let us **fix** our eyes on Jesus

G **Give** thanks to the LORD, for he is good!

H **How lovely** is your dwelling place

I **I am** the LORD your God

J The **joy** of the LORD is your strength

K **King** of kings and Lord of lords.

L The **LORD** is my rock and my fortress and my deliverer

M **My heart** and flesh sing for joy to the living God

N **Nothing** will be impossible with God

O   **Oh, clap** your hands, all you peoples!
        Shout to God with the voice of triumph!

P   **Prepare** the way of the LORD

Q   Do not **quench** the Spirit

R   **Remember** the wonders he has done

S   **Surely** your goodness and love
        will follow me all the days of my life

T   **This is** the day that the LORD has made

U   **Under** his wings you will find refuge

V   **Victory** belongs to the LORD

W   **Worthy is the Lamb**

X   How **excellent** is Your name in all the earth

Y   **Yours**, O LORD is the greatness
        Yours is the kingdom,

Z   And it was completely **calm**

WWW.FORTYFIVE.ONE
#ATO**Z**BIBLE

Printed in Great Britain
by Amazon